COPYRIGHT © 2023 RAMEESHAH SHAH
ALL RIGHTS RESERVED.

# TABLE OF CONTENTS

# APPLE

3

# ORANGE

4

# BANANA

5

# WATERMELON

6

# STRAWBERRY

7

# GRAPES

## (GREEN,RED,BLACK)

# PEACH

9

# RASPBERRY

# PINEAPPLE

# MANGO

12

# SWEET LIME

13

# PAPAYA

# GUAVA

15

# POMEGRANATE

16

# CUSTARD APPLE

# KIWI

18

# CHERRY

# CHIKU/ MANILKARA ZAPOTA

# MUSKMELON

21

# PASSION FRUIT

22

# DRAGON FRUIT

23

# PEAR

# LYCHEE

25

# PLUM

# FIG

27

# APRICOT

# GRAPEFRUIT

29

# MULBERRY

# BLUEBERRY

# DATES

# JACK FRUIT

33

# STAR FRUIT

34

# CRANBERRY

# MANGOSTEEN

36

# COCONUT

# AVOCADO

# RAMBUTAN

39

# LONGAN

40

# CANISTEL

41

# ROSE APPLE

42

www.ingramcontent.com/pod-product-compliance
Lightning Source LLC
Chambersburg PA
CBHW042055110726
48006CB00002B/406